PIANO / VOCAL / GUITAR

MERCYME
WELCOME TO THE NEW

ISBN 978-1-4803-9264-9

HAL•LEONARD® CORPORATION

7777 W. BLUEMOUND RD. P.O. BOX 13819 MILWAUKEE, WI 53213

Visit Hal Leonard Online at
www.halleonard.com

WELCOME TO THE NEW

Words and Music by BART MILLARD,
MIKE SCHEUCHZER, NATHAN COCHRAN,
ROBSHAFFER, BARRY GRAUL, SOLOMON OLDS,
DAVID GARCIA and BEN GLOVER

C#m   B

sounds so cra - zy now, __ but back then you could - n't see __ it.

A   G#7

But now here you are, __   eyes o - pen wide. __

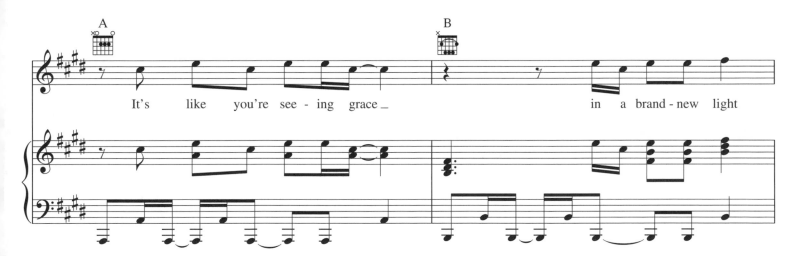

A   B

It's like you're see - ing grace __   in a brand - new light

E

for the first ___ time. Let us be the ___

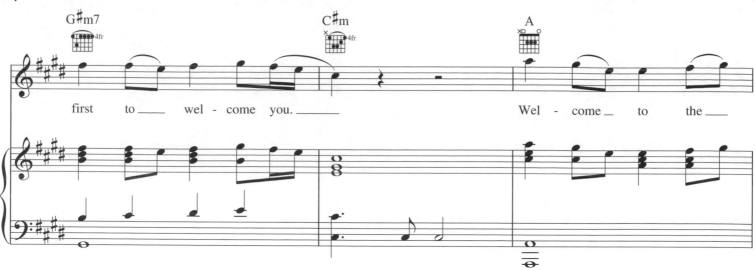

first to — wel - come you. — Wel - come — to the —

life you thought — was too good — to be true. —

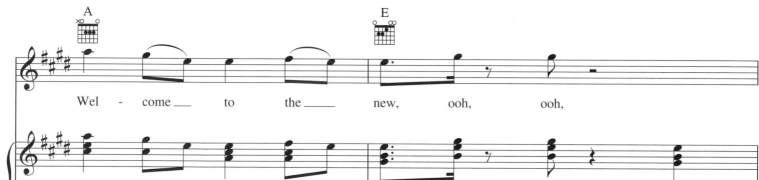

Wel - come — to the — new, ooh, ooh,

new, ooh, ooh, new, ooh, ooh.

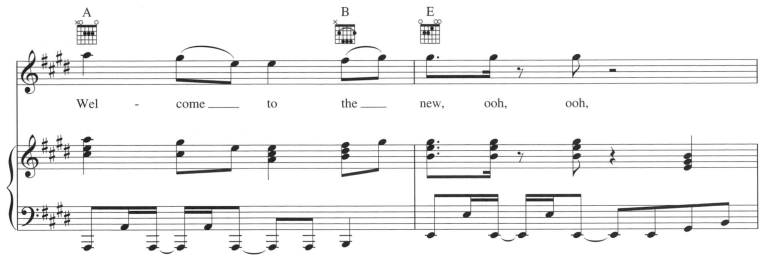

Wel - come ___ to the ___ new, ooh, ooh,

new, ooh, ooh, new, ooh, ooh.

To Coda

Wel - come ___ to the ___ new. You broke your back, kept all the rules, ___

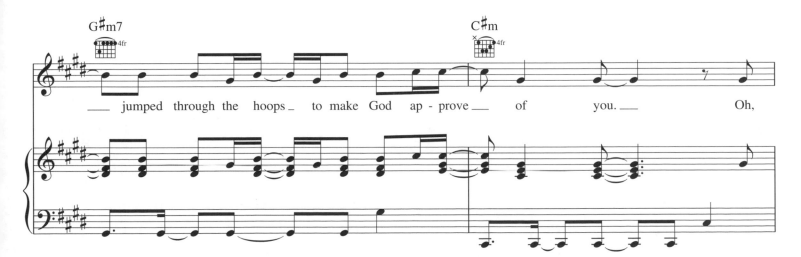

___ jumped through the hoops ___ to make God ap - prove ___ of you. ___ Oh,

tell me: was _ it worth _ it? The whole time you were spin - ning plates, _ did you

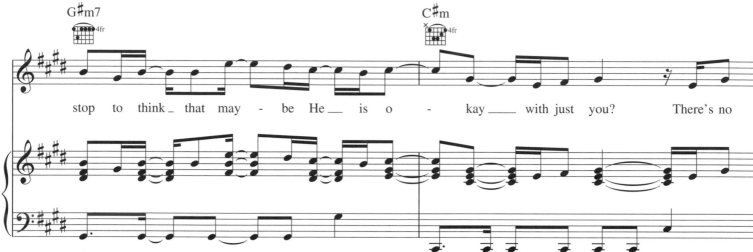

stop to think _ that may - be He _ is o - kay _ with just you? There's no

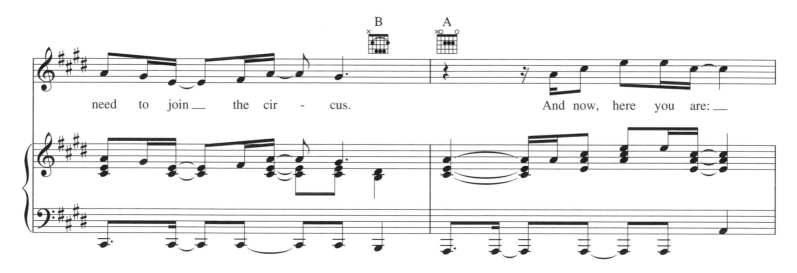

need to join _ the cir - cus. And now, here you are: _

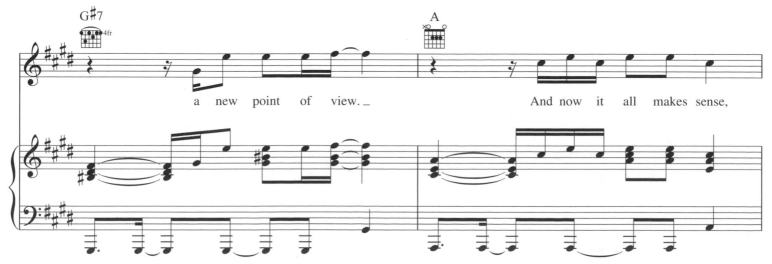

a new point of view. _ And now it all makes sense,

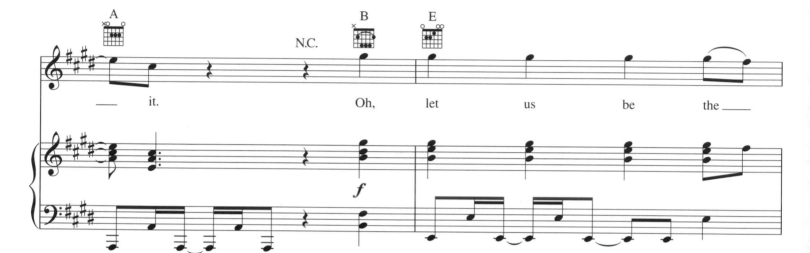

GOTTA LET IT GO

Words and Music by BART MILLARD,
MIKE SCHEUCHZER, NATHAN COCHRAN,
ROBSHAFFER, BARRY GRAUL, SOLOMON OLDS,
DAVID GARCIA and BEN GLOVER

Driving Rock

back at you.   It's   true,   but you can't

see   it 'cause you're stuck   on what you've been   through. _____   Hey!

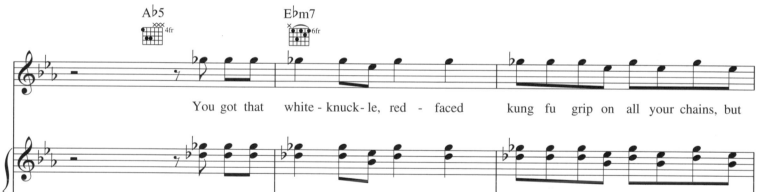

You got that   white - knuck - le, red - faced   kung fu grip on all your chains, but

that's   not   who you are.   I'm here to let you   know _

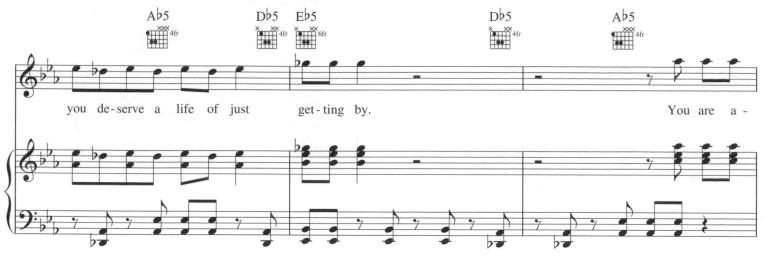

you de-serve a life of just get-ting by. You are a-

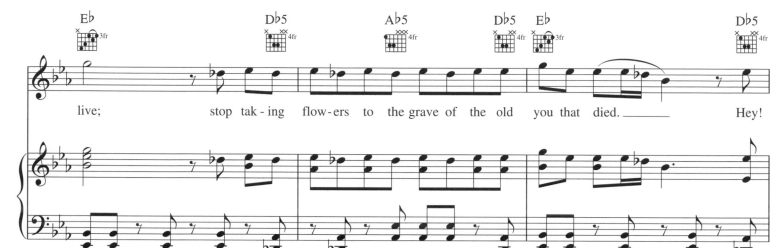

live; stop tak-ing flow-ers to the grave of the old you that died. _____ Hey!

If God can take your sin and free ya, for-get just like am-ne-sia, then

D.S. al Coda

why are you hold-ing on? I'm here to let you

CODA

Hey!

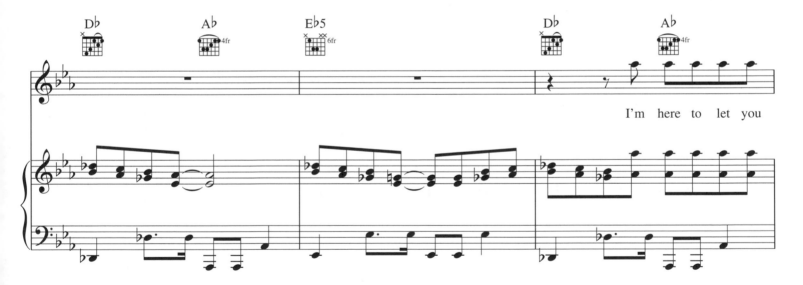

I'm here to let you

know __ you got-ta let it go. __

You were made for some-thing more, __ so come on and let it

go. __ Oh, __ oh, oh, __ oh, oh. __ Oh, __ oh, __ oh.

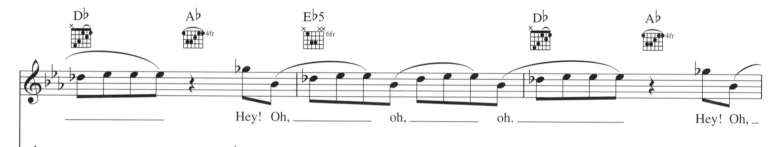

__ Hey! Oh, __ oh, __ oh. __ Hey! Oh, __

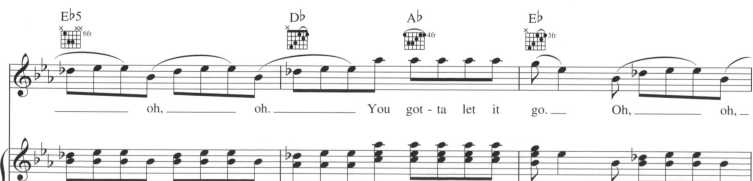

__ oh, __ oh. __ You got-ta let it go. __ Oh, __ oh, __

I'm here to let you_ know_ you got-ta let it_ go,_ you got-ta

let it_ go._ I'm here to

let you_ know_ you got-ta let it_ go,_ you got-ta

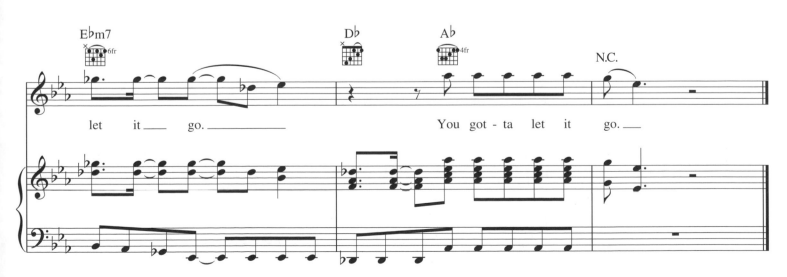

let it_ go._ You got-ta let it go._

SHAKE

Words and Music by BEN GLOVER, DAVID GARCIA,
SOLOMON OLDS, BART MILLARD,
MIKE SCHEUCHZER, NATHAN COCHRAN,
ROBSHAFFER and BARRY GRAUL

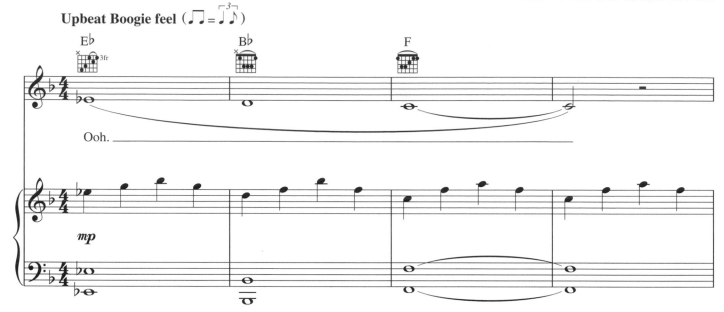

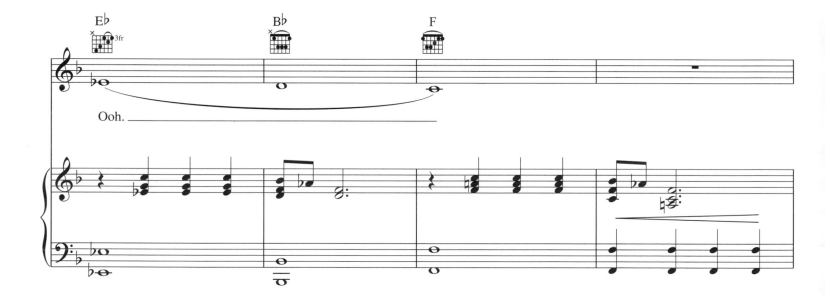

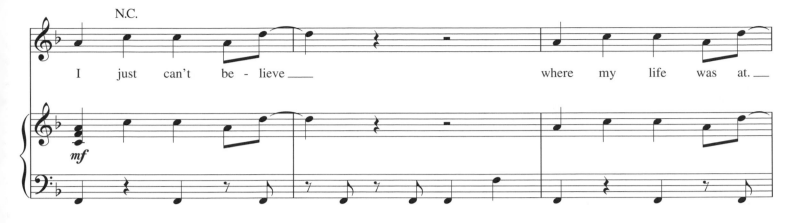

I just can't be-lieve ___ where my life was at. ___

___ All ___ that I know ___ is my heart ___ was broke, ___ and I don't ___

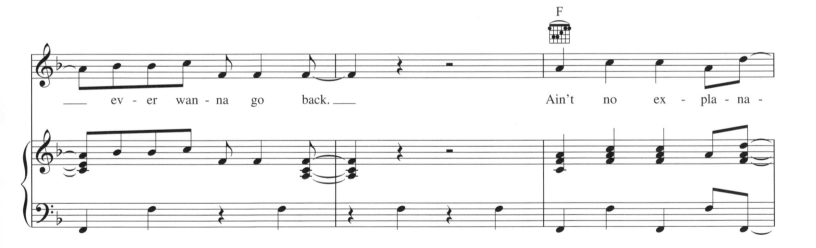

F

___ ev-er wan-na go back. ___ Ain't no ex-pla-na-

-tion how ___ I saw the light. ___ He ___

found me ___ and He set ___ me free, ___ and it brought ___ me back ___ to life. ___

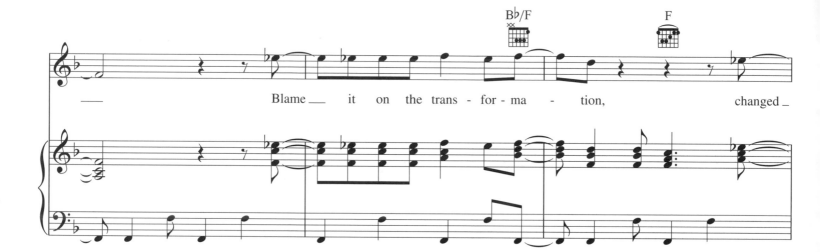

Bb/F   F

___ Blame ___ it on the trans - for - ma - tion, ___ changed ___

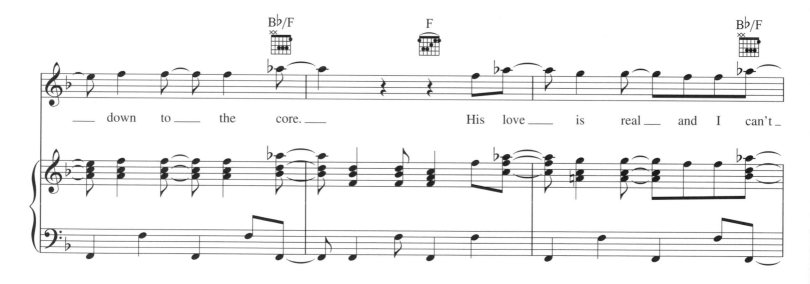

Bb/F   F   Bb/F

___ down to ___ the core. ___ His love ___ is real ___ and I can't ___

F   Bb/F   F

___ sit still ___ 'cause my name's ___ not shamed no more, ___ more, more. ___ Great ___

shake, (Shake!) shake ___ like you're changed. Shake, (Shake!) shake ___

___ like you're changed. May - be He came to you ___ when ev -

- 'ry - thing ___ seemed fine, ___ or may - be your world was up-

- side down; ___ it hit you right be - tween the eye, ___ eye, eyes. ___ No

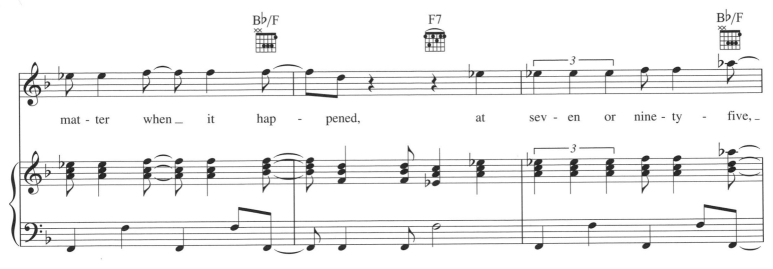

mat - ter when __ it hap - pened, at sev - en or nine - ty - five, __

__ move __ your feet __ 'cause you __ are free __ and you've nev -

- er been more a - live. _____ You got - ta shake, shake, shake __

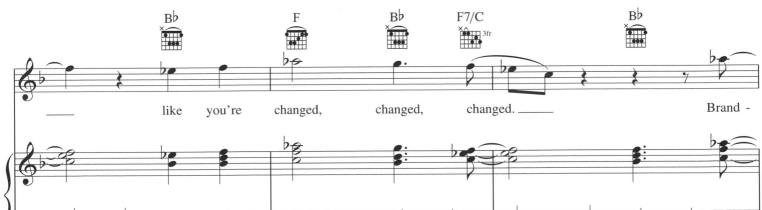

__ like you're changed, changed, changed. _____ Brand -

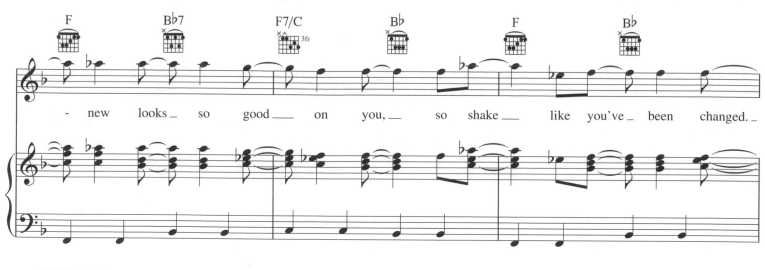

- new looks _ so good _ on you, _ so shake _ like you've _ been changed. _

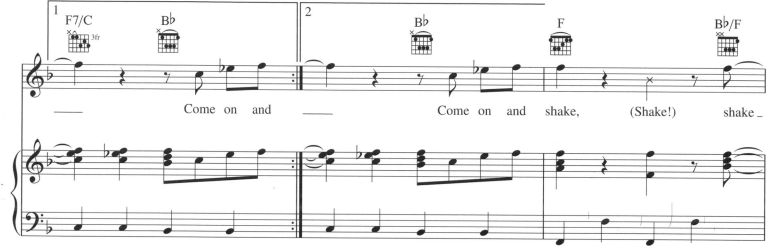

1 _ Come on and _ **2** Come on and shake, (Shake!) shake _

_ like you're changed. Shake, (Shake!) shake _ like you're changed.

(Shake!) (Shake!) Great _

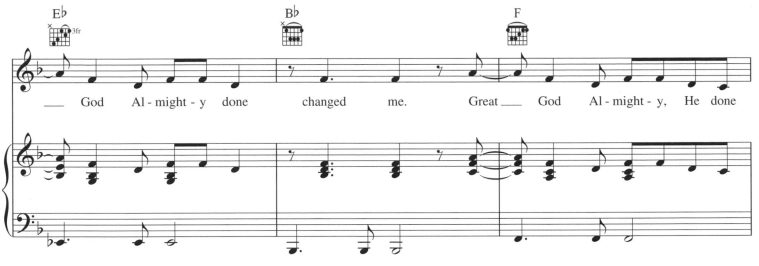

God Al-might-y done changed me. Great __ God Al-might-y, He done

changed me. Great __ God Al-might-y done changed me. Great __

__ God Al-might-y, He done changed me. No mat-ter when __ it hap-

-pened, at sev-en or nine-ty-five, ___ move __

your feet __ 'cause you __ are free __ and you've nev - er been more a - live. __

__ You've got to shake, shake, shake __ like you're changed, changed, changed. __

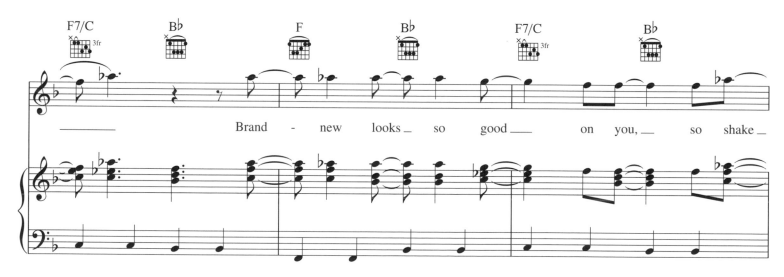

_____ Brand - new looks __ so good __ on you, __ so shake __

__ like you've __ been changed. __ Come on and ____ Come on and

shake, (Shake!) shake _____ like you're changed. Shake, (Shake!) shake _____

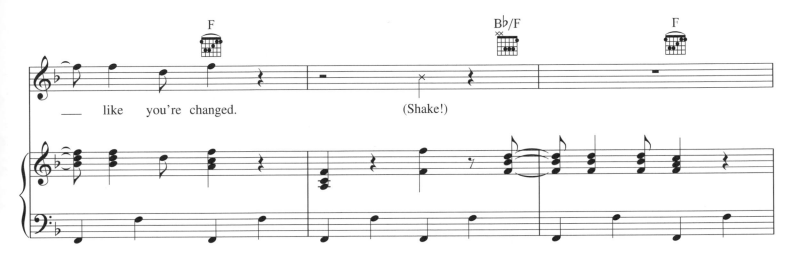

_____ like you're changed. (Shake!)

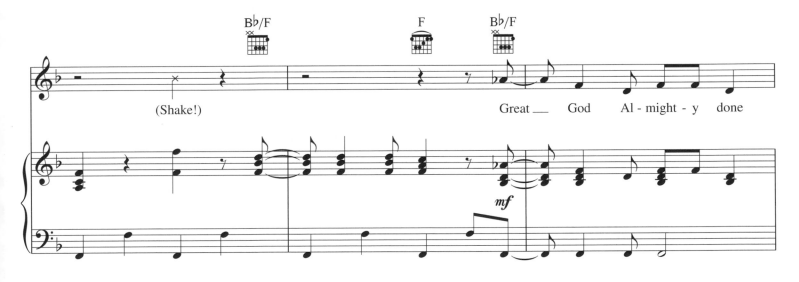

(Shake!) Great _____ God Al-might-y done

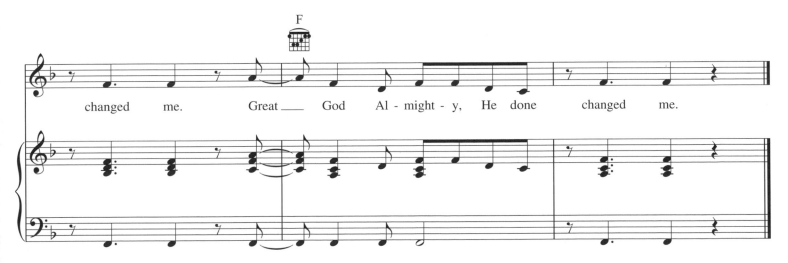

changed me. Great _____ God Al-might-y, He done changed me.

GREATER

Words and Music by BART MILLARD,
MIKE SCHEUCHZER, NATHAN COCHRAN,
ROBSHAFFER, BARRY GRAUL,
DAVID GARCIA and BEN GLOVER

Moderately fast

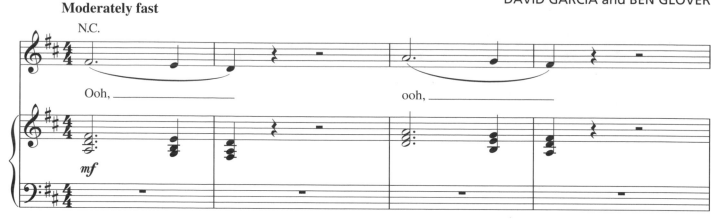

Ooh, _____ ooh, _____

ooh, _____ ooh. _____ Bring your

tired _____ and bring your shame, bring your guilt _____ and bring your
doubts _____ and bring your fears, bring your hurt _____ and bring your

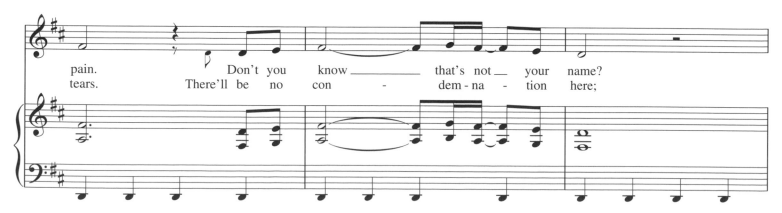

pain. Don't you know _____ that's not your name?
tears. There'll be no con - dem - na - tion here;

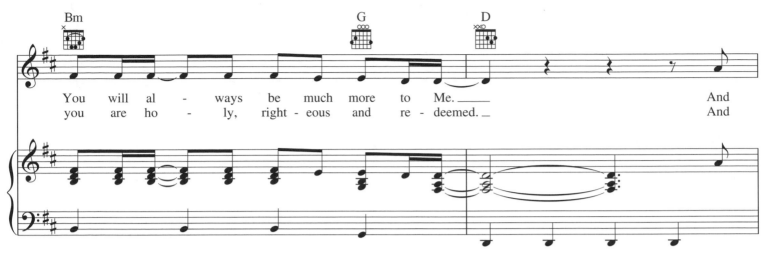

You will al - ways be much more to Me. _____ And
you are ho - ly, right - eous and re - deemed. _ And

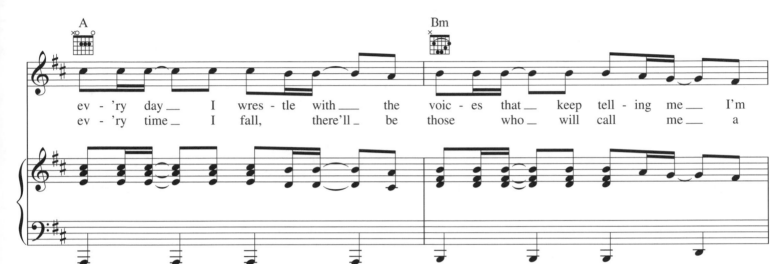

ev - 'ry day _ I wres - tle with _ the voic - es that _ keep tell - ing me _ I'm
ev - 'ry time _ I fall, there'll _ be those who _ will call me _ a

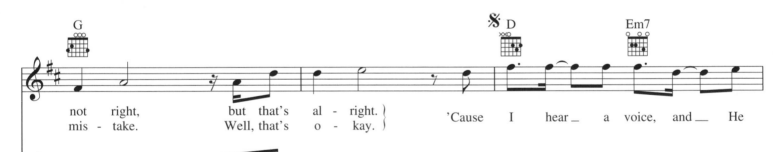

not right, but that's al - right. } 'Cause I hear _ a voice, and _ He
mis - take. Well, that's o - kay. }

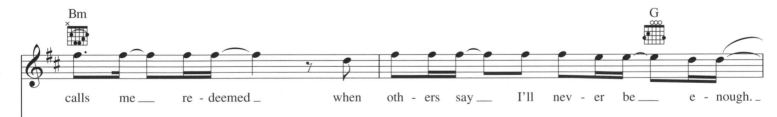

calls me _ re - deemed _ when oth - ers say _ I'll nev - er be _ e - nough. _

And great-er is ____ the One liv - ing

in - side ____ of me than he who ____ is liv - ing in the world, ____

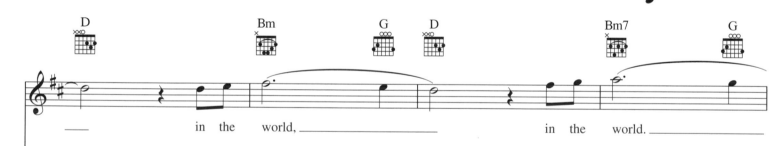

____ in the world, _____ in the world. _____

To Coda

And great-er is ____ the One liv - ing in - side ____ of me than

oh, _____ woo! Oh. _____

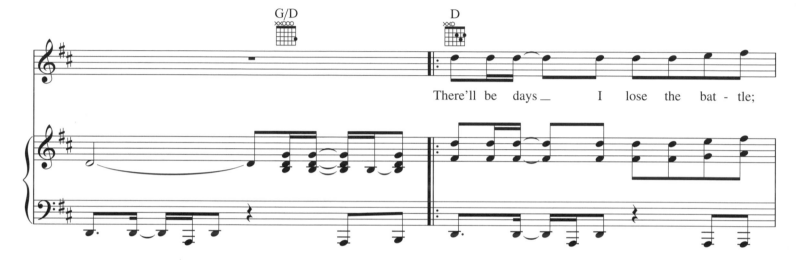

There'll be days __ I lose the bat - tle;

grace says __ that it does - n't mat - ter 'cause the cross __ al - read - y won the war. __

(He's great - er, He's great - er.)   I am learn - ing to run free - ly,

un-der-stand-ing just how He sees me, and it makes __ me love Him more and more. __

1

__ (He's great - er, He's great - er.)

2

__ (He's great - er, He's great - er.)

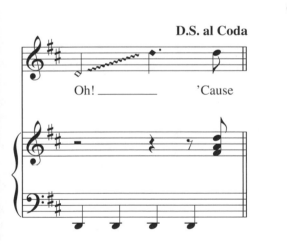

D.S. al Coda

Oh! _____ 'Cause

CODA

Bm7　　G　　D

he who __ is liv - ing in the world. __

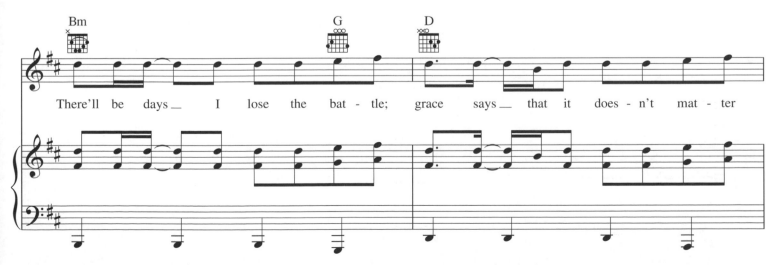

Bm　　G　　D

There'll be days __ I lose the bat - tle; grace says __ that it does - n't mat - ter

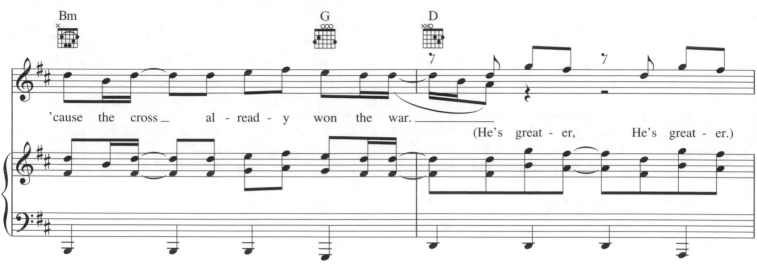

'cause the cross___ al-read-y won the war._____

(He's great-er, He's great-er.)

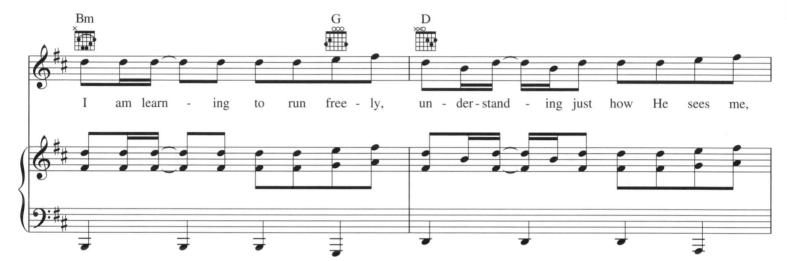

I am learn-ing to run free-ly, un-der-stand-ing just how He sees me,

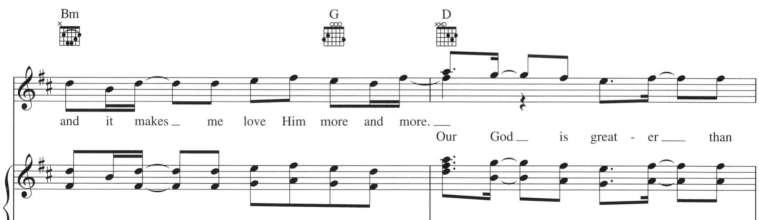

and it makes___ me love Him more and more.___

Our God___ is great-er___ than

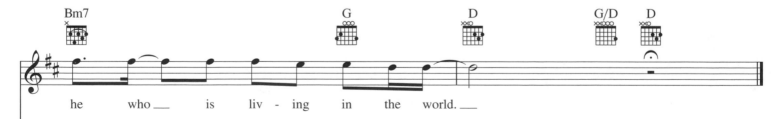

he who___ is liv-ing in the world.___

FINISH WHAT HE STARTED

Words and Music by BART MILLARD,
MIKE SCHEUCHZER, NATHAN COCHRAN,
ROBSHAFFER, BARRY GRAUL,
DAVID GARCIA and BEN GLOVER

Moderately slow Rock

and don't let it de-fine you. ___ Take heart; that's not

who you are. Our God is ___ a-ble, more than ca-pa-ble to be

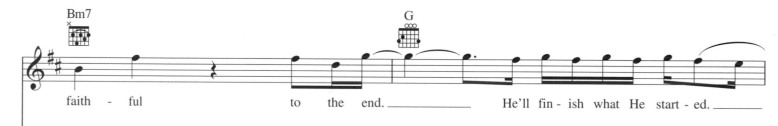

faith-ful to the end. ___ He'll fin-ish what He start-ed. ___

___ No mat-ter what ___ you've done, ___ grace ___ comes like ___ a flood. ___

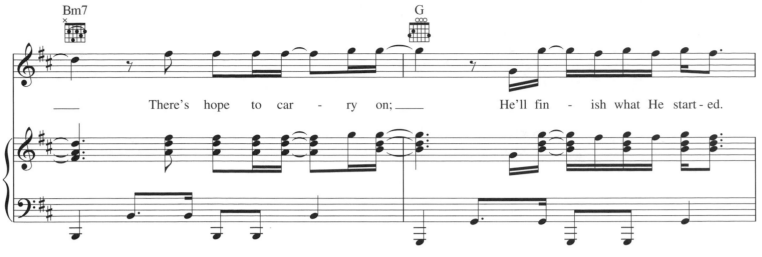

There's hope to car - ry on; ___ He'll fin - ish what He start - ed.

No mat - ter what ___ you face, ___ His mer - cy will ___ not change. ___

He's with ___ you all ___ the way; ___ He'll fin - ish what He start - ed. ___

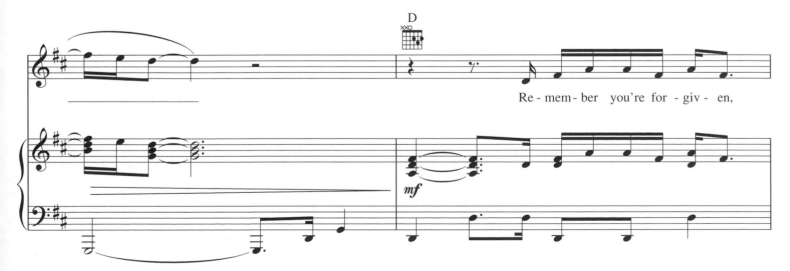

Re - mem - ber you're for - giv - en,

so there's no need to give in _____ to the lie that you're dis -

qual - i - fied. _____ Our God is _____

D.S. al Coda

CODA

_____ He'll fin - ish what He start - ed.

Oh, _____

oh. _____

This work He start - ed in you now, He's faith-ful to com-plete it.

The prom - ise was sealed when He cried out, "It is fin - ished!"

Oh, mm, oh. Oh, mm, oh.

Oh, mm, oh. He'll fin - ish what He start-ed,

No mat - ter what __ you've done, __ grace __ comes like __ a flood. __

__ There's hope to car - ry on; ___ He'll fin - ish what He start - ed. ___

__ No mat - ter what __ you face, __ His mer - cy will __ not change. __

__ He's with __ you all __ the way; __ He'll fin - ish what He start - ed, __

FLAWLESS

Words and Music by BART MILLARD,
MIKE SCHEUCHZER, NATHAN COCHRAN,
ROBSHAFFER, BARRY GRAUL, SOLOMON OLDS,
DAVID GARCIA and BEN GLOVER

Moderate Rock beat

There's got to be ___ more than go-ing back and forth, from do-ing right ___ ___ to do-ing wrong, ___ 'cause we were taught ___ that's who ___ we are. ___ Well, come on,

get in line _ right be-hind me, you a-long _ with ev-'ry-bod - y,

think-ing there's worth _ in what _ you _____ do.

Then, like a he-ro who takes _ the stage _ when we're on the edge of our seats _

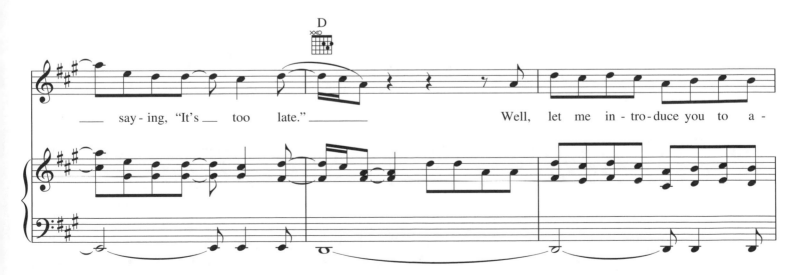

_____ say-ing, "It's _ too late." _____ Well, let me in-tro-duce you to a-

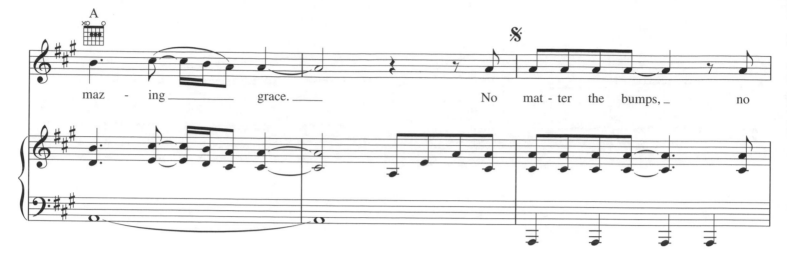

maz - ing _____ grace. _____ No mat - ter the bumps, _ no

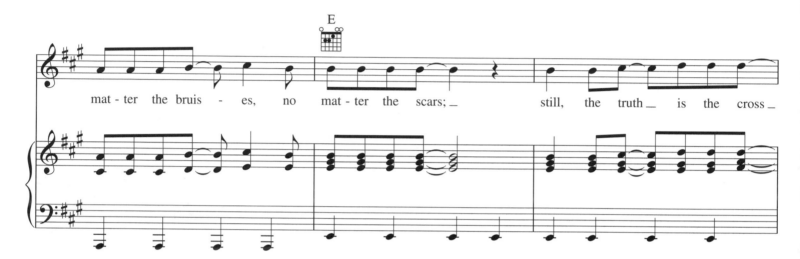

mat - ter the bruis - es, no mat - ter the scars; _ still, the truth _ is the cross _

_____ has made, _ the cross _ has made _ you flaw - less. (Cross _ has made _

_____ you _ flaw - less.) No mat - ter the hurt _ or how deep the wound _ is, no

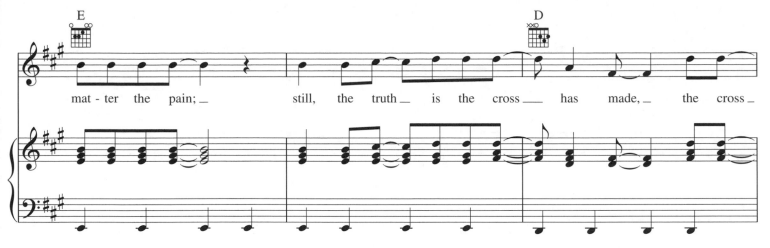

mat - ter the pain; _ still, the truth _ is the cross _ has made, _ the cross _

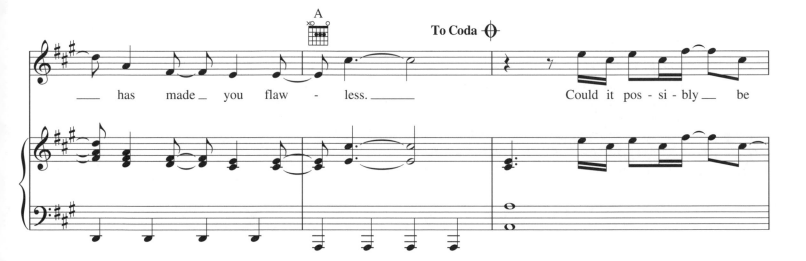

_ has made _ you flaw - less. _____ Could it pos - si - bly _ be

that we sim - ply can't be - lieve _ that ___ this

un - con - di - tion - al ___ kind of love ___ would be e - nough _____ to

take a filth - y wretch __ like this __ and wrap him up in right - eous - ness? __

D.S. al Coda

But that's ex - act - ly what __ He __ did. No

CODA

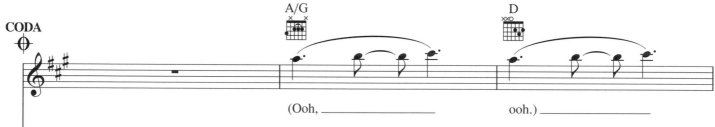

(Ooh, _____ ooh.) _____

Take a breath; smile __ and say, __ "Right here, right now, __ I'm __ o - kay __ be - cause __

the cross was __ e - nough." __

(Ooh, _____ ooh.) _____

And like a he - ro who takes __ the stage __ when we're

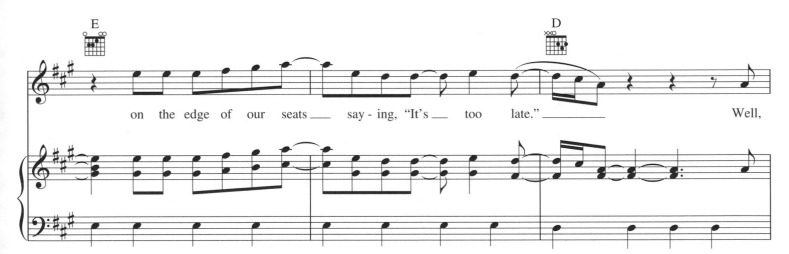

on the edge of our seats __ say - ing, "It's __ too late." _____ Well,

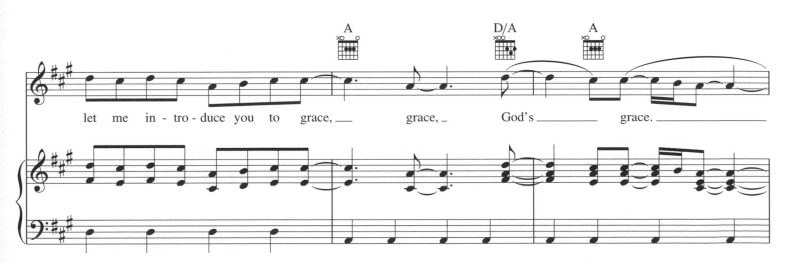

let me in - tro - duce you to grace, __ grace, _ God's _____ grace. _____

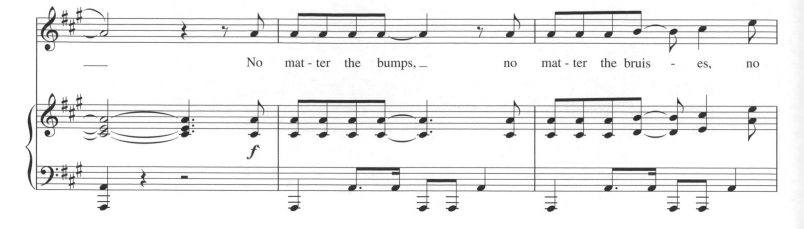

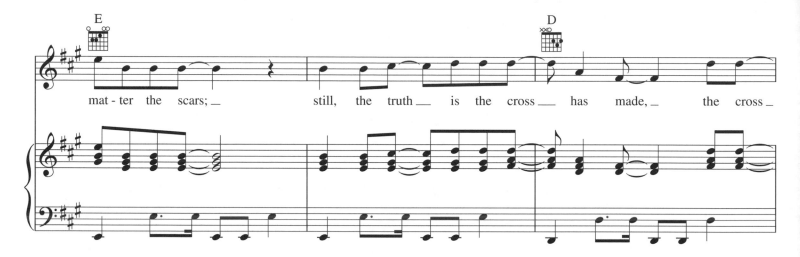

still, the truth ____ is the cross ____ has made, ____ the cross __

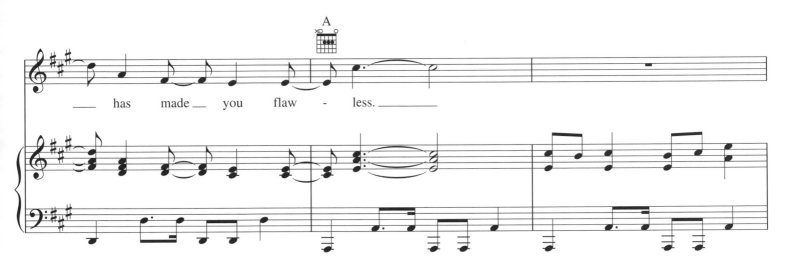

__ has made __ you flaw - less. ____

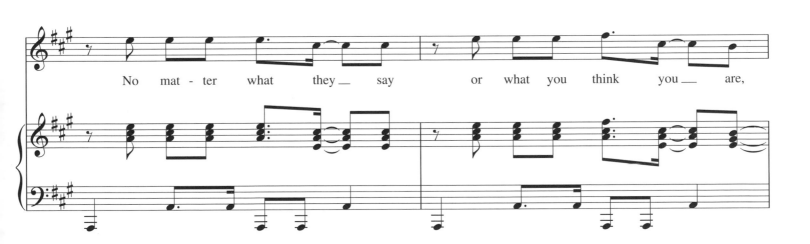

No mat - ter what they __ say or what you think you __ are,

the day you called His __ name He made ____ you ____ flaw -

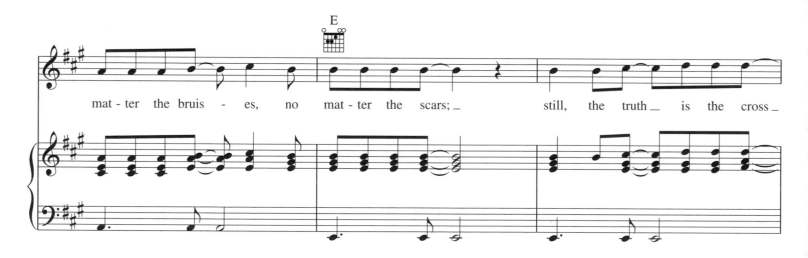

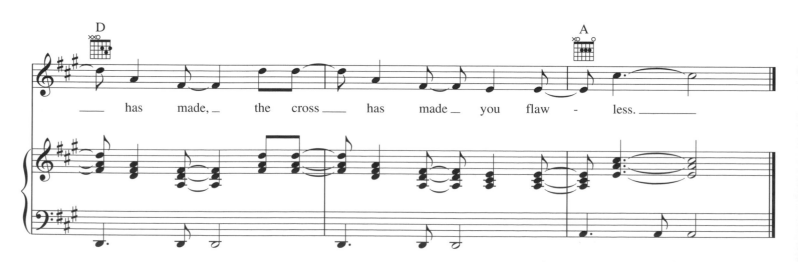

NEW LEASE ON LIFE

Words and Music by BART MILLARD,
MIKE SCHEUCHZER, NATHAN COCHRAN,
ROBSHAFFER, BARRY GRAUL, SOLOMON OLDS,
DAVID GARCIA and BEN GLOVER

Lyrics:

O Lord, have mer - cy ___ on this wea - ry ___ soul. ___ Come and take me to the riv - er ___ and make me whole. ___ It's down ___ with the old and up ___

_____ with the new. The hard ___ re - set: ___ my life, ___ take ___ two. _____

O Lord, have ___ mer - cy _____ on this wea - ry ___

_____ soul. I got a new lease on life. ___ They say you

on - ly live once, ___ but I live twice. _ I got a new lease on life. _

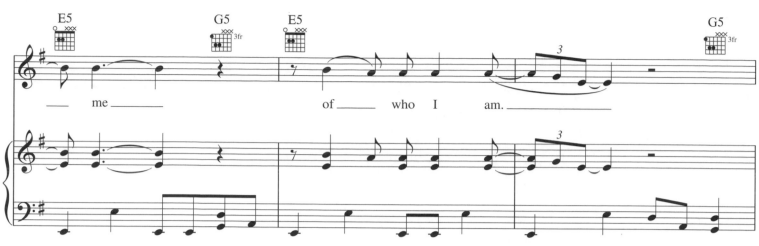

me _____ of _____ who I am. _____

My chains have been ____ shat - tered; _____ I'm a brand - new man. _

Well, I'm ____ free in - deed, I'm dead ____ no more, _ and at _

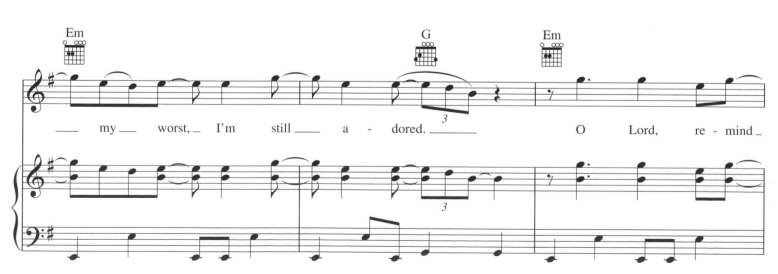

____ my ____ worst, _ I'm still ____ a - dored. _____ O Lord, re - mind _

D.S. al Coda

me: this is who I am. I got a

CODA

The en - e - my knows where I

call my home, but he's still try - ing to

mess up my life in the mean-time. So, ___ Lord, re - mind me:

Yeah, _____ yeah, _____ yeah. _____

_____ I got a new lease on life. _

___ They say you on - ly live ___ once, but I live twice. ___ I got a

WISHFUL THINKING

Words and Music by BART MILLARD,
MIKE SCHEUCHZER, NATHAN COCHRAN,
ROBSHAFFER, BARRY GRAUL,
DAVID GARCIA and BEN GLOVER

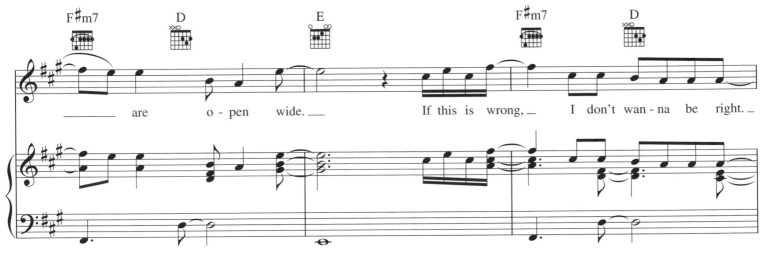

_____ are o-pen wide. ___ If this is wrong, __ I don't wan-na be right. __

___ Could it be that on my worst day, ___ how You love me still ___

will not change? _ What if it's real-ly not a-bout what I do, but what ___ You did? _

_____ Oh, what if _____ this ain't wish-ful think-ing, it's just

how it is, ___ this ain't wish-ful think-ing, it's just how it is? ___ Yeah.

Well, I ___

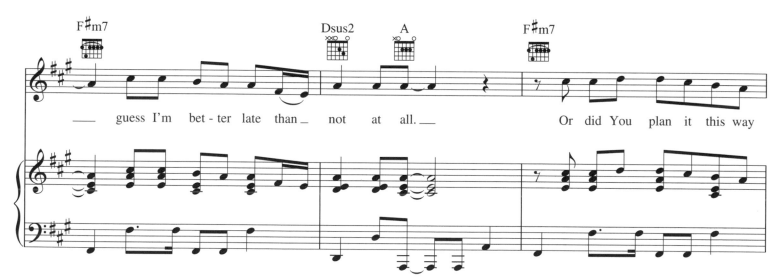

___ guess I'm bet-ter late than ___ not at all. ___ Or did You plan it this way

all a-long? ___ 'Cause with-out suf-fer-ing, grace is ___ hard to see. ___

So may-be I'm right where I'm s'posed__ to be.__ And__ now_____ I'm see-

- ing You so dif-fer-ent-ly.__ And all I can say___ is,__ "Fi - nal - ly!" Yeah.

Could it be____ that on my worst day, ___ how You love me sim-ply

will not change?__ What if it's real-ly not a-bout what I do, but what___ You did?__

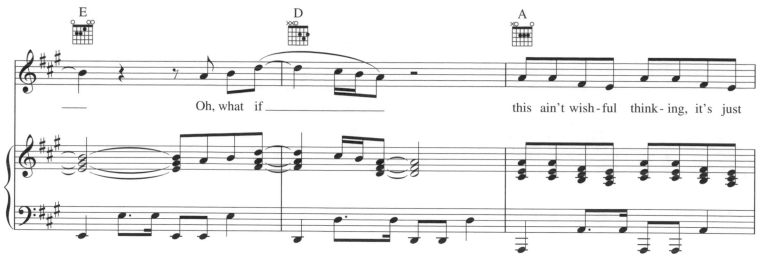

Oh, what if _____ this ain't wish-ful think-ing, it's just

how it is, ___ this ain't wish-ful think-ing, it's just how it is? ___ It's how it is. ___

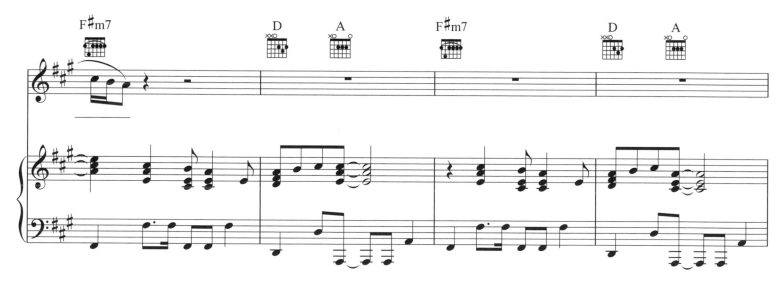

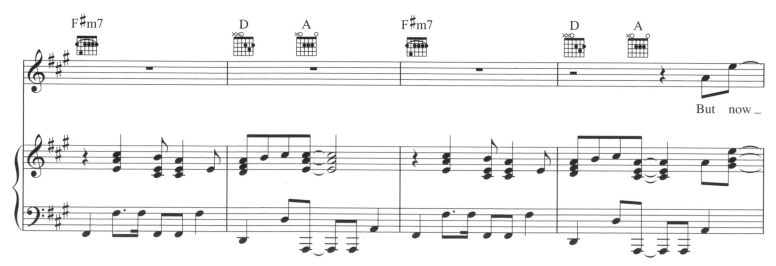

But now _

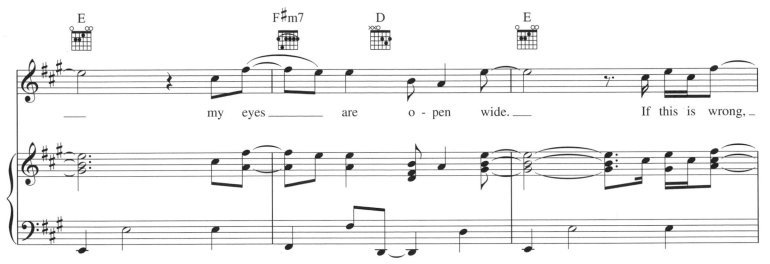

my eyes _____ are o - pen wide. ___ If this is wrong, _

___ Lord, don't make me, don't You make me right. _____ Ooh. _

Oh, _____ whoa. _____ Hey, _____ now, ___ hey - ey - ey - ey -

ey. Now I know _ that on my worst day, (my worst day) ___ the way You love me, it ain't

never gon-na change. ___ It's nev-er real-ly been a-bout what I do, but what ___ You did. ___

___ Oh yes, it is. _____ This ain't wish-ful think-ing, it's just

how it is. ___ This ain't wish-ful think-ing, it's just how it is. ___

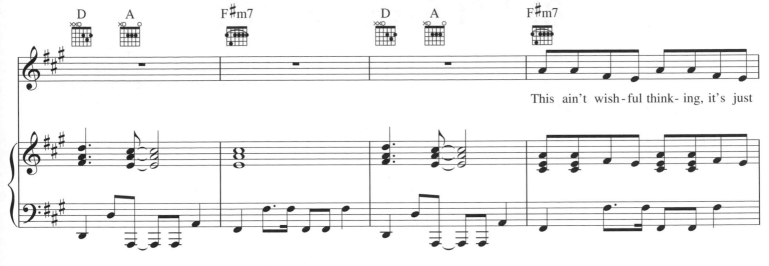

This ain't wish-ful think-ing, it's just

how it is.___ This ain't wish-ful think-ing, it's just how it is.___

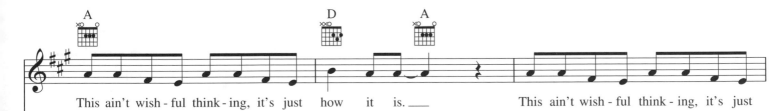

This ain't wish-ful think-ing, it's just how it is.___ This ain't wish-ful think-ing, it's just

how it is.___ This ain't wish-ful think-ing, it's just how it is.___

BURN BABY BURN

Words and Music by BART MILLARD,
MIKE SCHEUCHZER, NATHAN COCHRAN,
ROBSHAFFER, BARRY GRAUL, SOLOMON OLDS,
DAVID GARCIA and BEN GLOVER

Driving Rock beat

And do we know ex-act-ly who we are? _____
And do we know ex-act-ly what we have? _____

_____ We hold the light, _ but we
_____ Why don't we let _____ it _____

still lis-ten to the dark. _____
shine while we have the chance? _____

And it tells _____
It's not _____

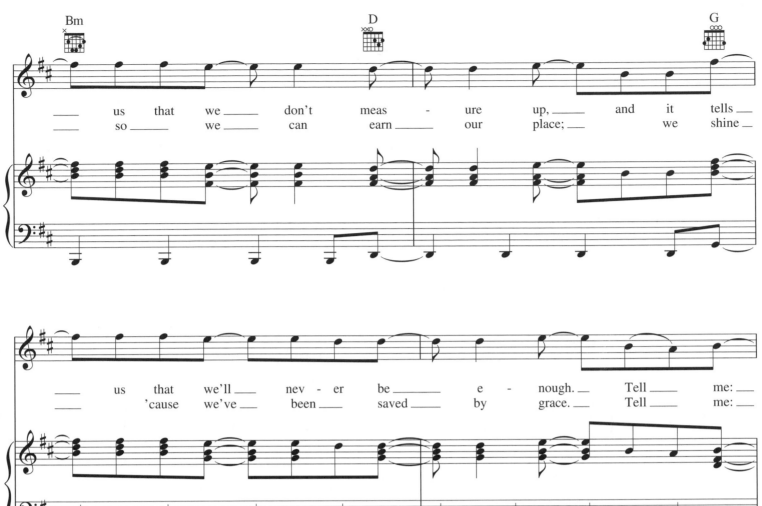

Bm **D** **G**

us that we ___ don't meas - ure up, ___ and it tells ___
so ___ we ___ can earn ___ our place; ___ we shine ___

us that we'll ___ nev - er be ___ e - nough. ___ Tell ___ me: ___
'cause we've ___ been saved ___ by grace. ___ Tell ___ me: ___

Bm **D** **G** **D/F♯**

do we know ex - act - ly who we are? ___ }
do we know ex - act - ly what we have? ___ }

G **D** **Em7**

We ___ are the light, ___ light ___ of the world; ___

light _ up the night. _ When _ will we learn? _ Now _ is our time, _

now _ is our turn _____ to burn, _ ba - by, burn, ba - by.

(Whoa.) _____ Burn, _

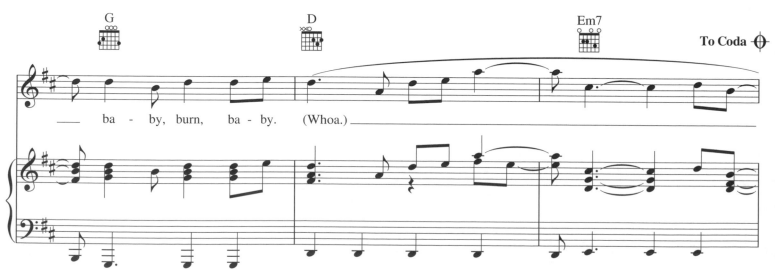

_ ba - by, burn, ba - by. (Whoa.) _____

To Coda ⊕

Burn, ___ ba - by, burn, ba - by.

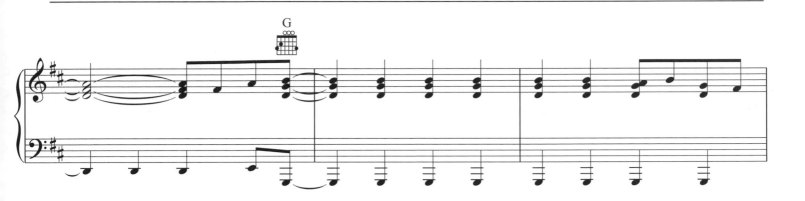

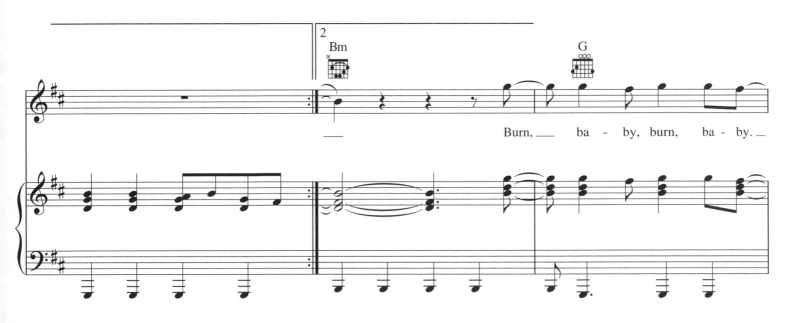

Burn, ___ ba - by, burn, ba - by. ___

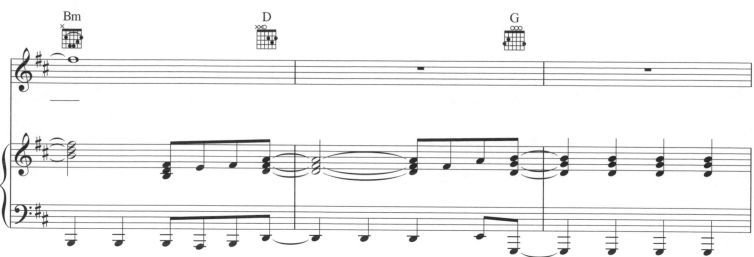

Oh, we're a cit - y on ___ a hill -

- side so ___ bright; keep ___ on shin - ing. Oh,

D.S. al Coda

take that fire ___ from the in - side out - side; keep ___ on burn - ing.

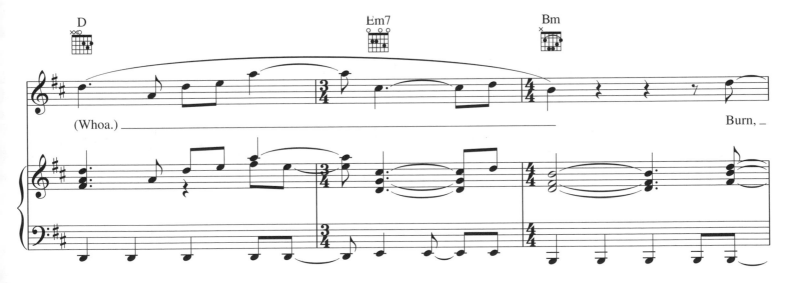

DEAR YOUNGER ME

Words and Music by BART MILLARD,
MIKE SCHEUCHZER, NATHAN COCHRAN,
ROBSHAFFER, BARRY GRAUL,
DAVID GARCIA and BEN GLOVER

Dear young-er me, _____ where

do I start? _____ If I could tell _____ you ev-'ry-thing _ that I _____

_____ have learned _ so far, _ then you could be _____ one

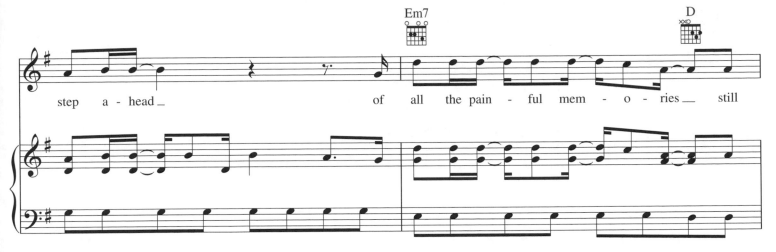

step a-head __ of all the pain - ful mem - o - ries __ still

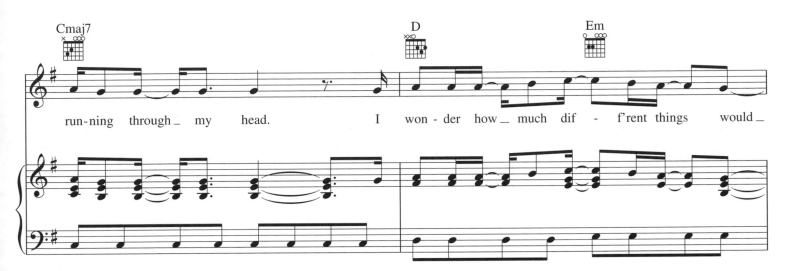

run-ning through __ my head. I won - der how __ much dif - f'rent things would __

__ be. Dear young - er me. __

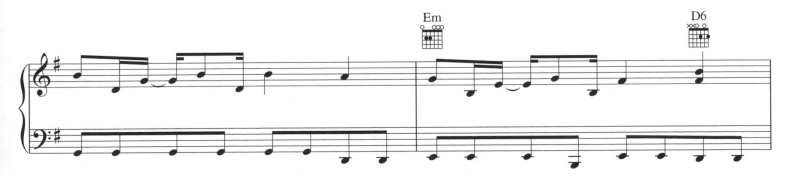

Dear young-er me, ____ I can -

not de - cide: _ do I give some speech a - bout _ how to get the most _

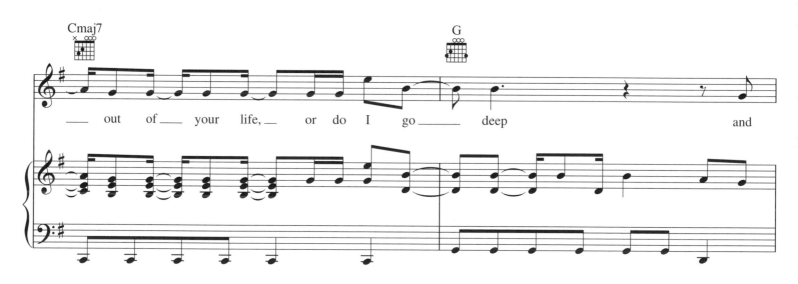

_ out of _ your life, _ or do I go _____ deep and

try to change _ the choic - es that _ you'll make? _ 'Cause they're _ the choic -

-es that __ made me. And e - ven though __ I love __ this cra -

- zy life, __ some - times I wish __ it was __ a smooth - er ride. __

Dear young - er me. __

Dear young - er me. __

_____ knew then _ what I _ know now, _ would -'ve not been hard to fig - ure out _ what I _

_____ would -'ve changed if I _____ had heard: _

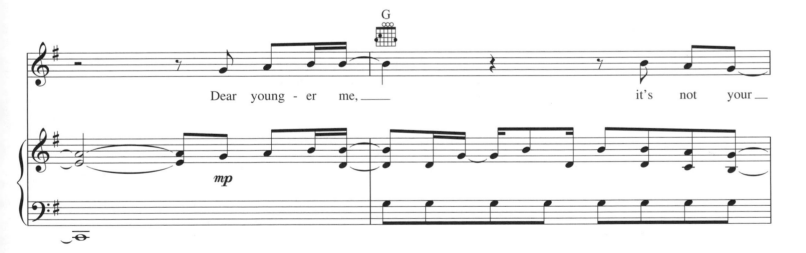

Dear young - er me, _____ it's not your _

_____ fault; you were nev - er meant _ to car - ry this _

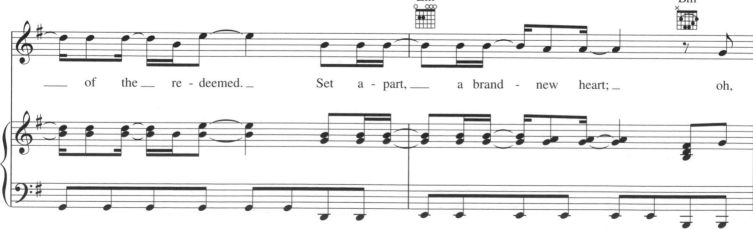

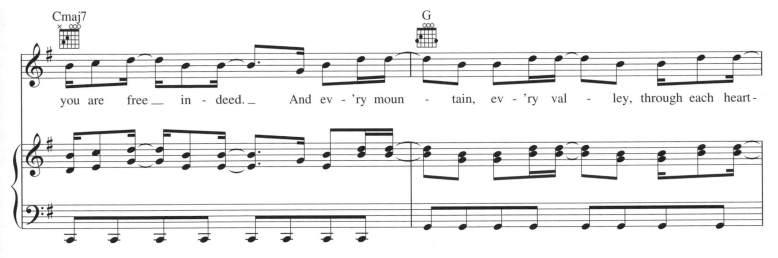

you are free __ in - deed. __ And ev - 'ry moun - tain, ev - 'ry val - ley, through each heart-

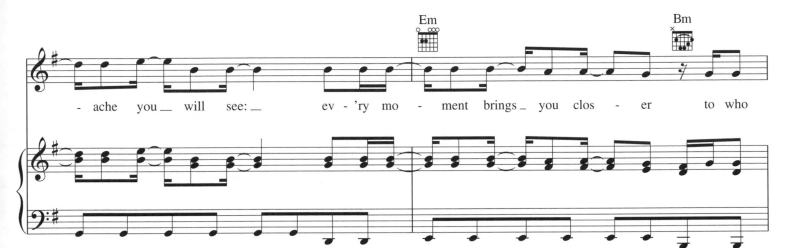

- ache you __ will see: __ ev - 'ry mo - ment brings __ you clos - er to who

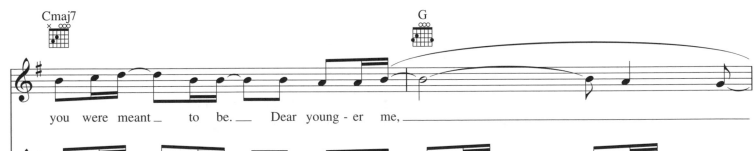

you were meant __ to be. __ Dear young - er me, _____

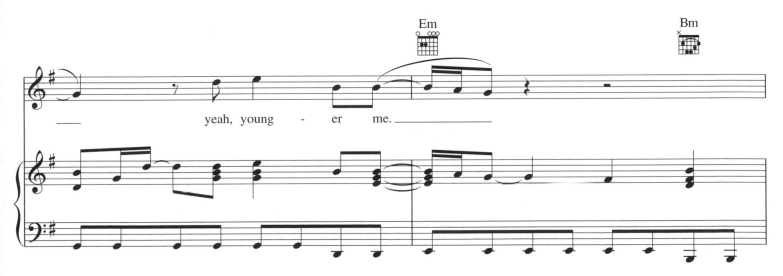

_____ yeah, young - er me. _____